liminal

liminal

a refugee memoir

LIMINAL
a refugee memoir

First Edition 2018

© 2018 by Liyah Babayan
Cover Design © 2018 Sergio Larios
Grammatical & Structural Edit by Vonia Jackson
Printed in the United States of America

All rights reserved.

No part of this publication may be reproduced, stored in a retrieval system, or transmitted in any form or by any means (including electronic, mechanical, photocopying, recording, or otherwise) without prior written permission,
except for quotations in articles or book reviews.

ISBN-10: 0615649653

For information about custom editions,
booking events, and wholesale purchases,
contact Liyah Babayan at
Facebook.com/liminalmemoir or
P. O. Box 5762, Twin Falls, Idaho, 83303 USA

In honor of my grandparents and parents who raised me to be proud, brave and compassionate. I am humbled by the unconditional support of all the backers of LIMINAL. My deepest gratitude goes to my platinum backers Edik Fandunyan and Sergio Larios. A special thank you to my family and the following Kickstarter supporters:

Bassam Kassab

Ray Yomtob

Yavruian Family

Susan Lopker Reitsma

Dale B. Atkinson

Jeanne Alban

Nurveta Bektic

Armen Gyurdzhiyants

Steve & Alana Caward

James K Miansian

Kevin and Kim Rosenau

Vladimir Danilyants

Patty and Gerry Freire

Svetlana Craddock

Bonnie & Art Hoag

A note to my son and daughter:

If I must choose one lesson to instill in you my dearest Dominic and Angeli, it is, without hesitation and most importantly the lesson of compassion. For as much justice sustains the rule of law society we enjoy, it is compassion "justice of the heart" that will keep you sincerely responsible to the human race and protective of all life. Always remember my darlings, that, what is ethical is not always legal and what is legal is not always ethical. It is my prayer that your heart knows the difference.

Mama

I write this for my refugee family.
I write this for the displaced people of the world. I write this for those who have become invisible and voiceless. I write this for those who know and can't deny the depths of their wounds. I write this for those who cannot write it themselves. I write this for those who are still afraid to. I write this for those who are persecuted and killed for their faith. I write this for those who will never know justice. I write this for those who cannot forget. I write this for those who live with the scars of genocide. I write this for those who know oppression, injustice, hate speech, discrimination, and persecution first hand. I write this for those who left what they knew to rebuild their entire life out of absolutely nothing. I write this for those who never forgot their roots. I write this for those who have been stripped of their humanity, identity and labeled "disposable" or "casualty of war". I write this for all the children of war. I write this for those who live with PTSD. I write this for those who have been dehumanized, abused, tortured, terrorized, persecuted, hated, force out of their homes, out of their motherland, off their continent and rescued, relocated and adopted by America. I write this for those who rebuild their entire life with the crumbs of the American Dream.

Liyah Babayan

Liminal (from the Latin word Imen,) meaning "a threshold," is the point of transitional time or condition in which one, or a group, or a territory, is not what it was and not what it will become, but something in between, something marginal, vague and flexible.

liminal

a refugee memoir

Authored by Liyah Babayan
Edited by Sergio Larios

PREFACE

In fourth grade, I got into a fight with a boy, Cody, I punched him straight in the nose. The outside ground teacher told my classroom teacher, Ms. Gunter, and I was in trouble. Ms. Gunter asked me what happened, but since I did not know English very well, I could not explain myself. Feeling helpless and scared, I watched Cody tell his side of the story pointing his finger at me the whole time. As he stood across from me with his nose tucked into his bloody tissue, crying, all the attention was on the weird, foreign, refugee girl who punched him.

Ms. Gunter asked me why I hit Cody. I could not explain to her that he and another girl have been harassing and doing mean things to me for weeks. Tripping me in the hall, putting boogers in my hair, telling me I stink and yelling in front of other students "Go back to your country!" The girl's parents got a restraining order against me, even though she was the one harassing me. I was told I could not play anywhere on the playground where she and her friends played.

Even if I could speak English, who would believe me anyway? After weeks of shoving me, tripping me and yelling in my face I decided to stand up for myself. So, this time, when Cody told me to go back to my country, I punched him straight in the face. As punishment, I was to stay inside during recess for a week when everyone went to play outside. My parents were never notified of any wrongdoing; they did not know about any restraining order and Cody did not get in trouble at all.

Ms. Gunter understood what happened, even though I could not tell her exactly. I started to cry because I felt like a mute, unable to communicate with anyone. I missed my family, and living where I could speak the language and where people understood me. Adjusting to a new school had its challenges, but even more when adjusting to a new culture at the same time. She probably sensed I was feeling scared about being new in this country. She noticed I was isolated most of the time and how some kids made fun of me. She asked me how I felt after I punched Cody. I answered, in my limited English, "I feel proud". Ms. Gunter smiled and gave me a warm, long hug.

The next day, I sat at my desk watching the rest of my classmates play at recess through the windows. Ms. Gunter sat down next to me and showed me a book. She showed me the pictures first and then started telling me about a girl who lived during a war I never heard of. The girl's name was Anne Frank. For the next few days, Ms. Gunter read to me out of this book, and I understood very little. I stared at her picture, I felt a connection to Anne Frank. For once, I felt I was not alone, that other children, other families experienced war like my family and the feeling of being unwanted. Ms. Gunter gifted me a little notebook. She encouraged me to write about my thoughts and feelings, as I was beginning to learn English. So I did, documenting my and my family's refugee experience.

I compiled the writings from my years of journaling as a child refugee growing up in America into this memoir. Much of my early journal entries are in extreme broken and elementary English, very difficult to understand. In my later teen years, my grasp of English came to be a little more developed. I would like to capture this language-learning phase of my integration in America through my (English-in-Progress) style in this memoir. In tribute to my younger, less articulate, English learner self - as well as to bring awareness to the limitations language learners face in their everyday communication in a new country.

I prepare the readers in advance for language-in-progress expressions throughout the chapters. I include journal entries from early on when I just started to learn English. Leaving them in the original integrity, with intention to honor my childhood voice in full. This memoir reflects on my life before coming to America 1983-1992 and after arriving to America 1992-2002. I began journaling in English in 1994, continuing all the way through my adolescent years into now adulthood.

I am forever grateful to Ms. Gunter for turning a punishment into an opportunity to welcome and heal a refugee child. For the gift of writing, for fostering my inner voice and preparing me for my new life in America.

1

Compassionate Response

"It (genocide) killed us inside, like this we are still living."

(journal entry - age 11)

The image from the 12th floor of my home in Baku, Azerbaijan has haunted me all my child and adult life. I watched from our balcony, as tens of thousands of Azerbaijani men gather in the boulevard, chanting to cleanse the city of Armenians. In absolute fear, my Mama grabbing me away from the balcony, turning off the lights. Ethnic killings of Armenians began on February 27, 1988, in the city of Sumgait, just 18 miles away from the capital Baku, where we lived. After the massive rally in Baku, the men were given lists, addresses of Armenian neighborhoods, homes and places of employment. Immediately my family went into hiding.

The ethnic violence promised and planned by Azeri political leaders in advance was in direct retaliation against the demands of Nagorno-Karabakh Armenians to secede from Azerbaijian. No one was spared in Baku, it was complete anarchy. Tens of thousands of Armenians were brutally tortured, sodomized, ripped apart, burned alive. Pregnant women, toddler girls, women and grandmothers gang raped as our brothers, fathers, husbands forced to watch. Women forced to dance in the streets naked, then drenched in gasoline and set on fire alive. The unborn carved out of their mothers' wombs, babies smashed against sidewalks. (Forgive me for sharing details... I live with these memories.) My loved ones, stabbed, beaten, tortured, raped, thrown off buildings alive and their bodies mutilated. Over 300,000 Armenians were purged out of their homes, grabbing what they can carry fleeing for safety. This is how my family became refugees, this is what we miraculously survived.

This horror repeats in my mind. Growing up with flashbacks, triggers, anxiety and survivor's guilt, I struggled to grip to reality and function. I could not talk about that which I could not understand. My entire family has internalized the violence we survived, we don't talk about it. We live with this trauma. I function. We function. I function to survive. We function to survive. We go on, rebuilding our life best we can, living with Chronic Post Traumatic Stress Disorder. War and genocide are not something the human psyche can just "deal with." It killed us inside, like this we are still living.

My family was brought to America in 1992, resettled by the College of Southern Idaho Refugee Program to Twin Falls, a city in the state of Idaho. Immediately after arriving as refugees, my parents were hurried into lowest wage employment, my brother and I placed in public schools. Our family thrown into a new society and expected to "assimilate" on our own. Expected to start a new life without any information, resources or support to navigate a society, a government, laws, economy and a culture completely new to us. Disturbed by the ethnic killings we experienced and culture shock on top of what we just survived, only compounded our trauma. We had no space, no time, no opportunity to heal individually, or as a family.

Refugees face the intense stress of rebuilding our entire life in a new country without resources to manage our trauma from living through a horrific war, massacre, torture, rape, loss of family members...with only a few hours of orientation, a job and the pressure to become self-sufficient as soon as possible. They expect us to learn English at the same time we are learning to survive. They expect us to know the laws and norms of a new land. They expect us to understand the legal system and other institutions. They expect us to know our individual and Constitutional rights. They expect us to be perfectly mentally, emotionally and physically well after surviving extreme violence and war. They expect us to navigate through the culture shock and culture clash on our own. They expect us to become "American," stop feeling our past and form a new identity overnight, but how can we?

We experience prejudice and persecution, sometimes violence in our adoptive communities, as we do during the conflicts we flee. Refugees are a resilient population, because we survive everything, we have the extraordinary spirit to survive anything. Of course the refugee resettlement program is a noble response, a humanitarian and much needed agency to rescue displaced humanity. It lacks however, by nature of the program funding, the ability to address the mental, emotional and psychological needs of the traumatized men, women and children it's designed to resettle. More accurately, the U.S. Refugee Resettlement Program functions more as modern day, legal form of cheap labor pipeline to the communities which host them.

My hope in sharing my family's refugee experience is to bring attention to the dire reform needed to resettlement programs, and inspire compassionate response in the adoptive communities that resettle refugees. There is more to the resettlement of men, women and children than fronting an airplane ticket and hustling refugees, who just survived war and genocide, to the lowest paying job sites.

Refugees are human beings, they are not objects, cases, documents or the crisis they escaped. The intention to rescue the whole human, not just the laborer, requires compassionate response to their compounded trauma, experienced violence and the cultural shock of a new country.

2

Earliest Memory

"I don't want my friends to know about my real childhood. It is where I hide the rest of me, the part I cannot talk about."

(journal entry - age 12)

My earliest life memory is playing on the beach as a child. Spending summers with all my family and relatives cooking shish kebabs on the beaches of the Caspian Sea. My little fingers sweeping through the warm sand, finding sea shells, the smell of salt sea air and shish kebab. The sounds of waves, music, nardi (backgammon) dice rolling across game boards and adults laughing. Feeling the hot sun on my skin, playful, careless days and free of concern. Eating fresh fruit and sweets, surrounded by all my family, playing with my cousins. Sweet and innocent, as childhood memories should be.

When I reflect back on my childhood to find comfort in pure and good memories, the only one that is not tainted by evil is this one memory. I hold on to it as vividly as I can, I treasure this childhood memory, it is sacred to me. This is the only "normal" memory of childhood I have to share with my friends when talking about my past. When other children talk about their childhood, I feel sad, wishing I could relate to their experience. I feel scared and embarrassed to talk about mine. I don't want my friends to know about my real childhood. It is where I hide the rest of me, the part I cannot talk about. The only memory I have of my family whole, happy and safe is before the (pogroms) organized massacre began. Before we started to live in fear. Before the violence. Before we were hunted.

Paternal Grandmother Gohar (Gyanzhuntsev Arshakovna) Babayan (Baku)

My Father (bottom center) along with his siblings and my Grandmother Gohar (Baku, 1951)

My Grandfather Sarkiss honored on Victory Day, May 9th as a WWII MIA/POW

3

Hereditary Genocide

"My black hair and features always remind me of the Genocide. I often felt this pain and shame in looking in the mirror, I feel my ancestors."

(journal entry - age 14)

Both my parents, my brother and I were born and raised in Baku, Azerbaijan. Even though we were ethnic Armenian, back then it did not matter in what republic you were born in, it was all the Soviet Russian Empire. We were all Soviet citizens. To us our history and ethnicity was our identity, not the borders drawn around us throughout wars and politics. Armenians are indigenous people who trace their long history and heritage to Noah's Ark and his sons on Mount Ararat. In 301, Arsacid Armenia was the first sovereign nation to accept Christianity as a state religion. Armenians surviving religious persecution, when forced out of their historic lands, settled in neighboring territories throughout the South Caucasus and Middle East.

My father's side of the family is from the historic Armenian land of Nagorni Karabak (Artsah, Արցախ) and when they migrated to the coastal area near the Caspian Sea, the territory, language and ethnicity "Azerbaijan" did not yet exist. The Silk Roads, ancient trade routes connecting Asia and Europe, passed through several cities in the north-western direction through this region. Baku, the coastal capital, located on the crossroads of the East and West, has always been and even today remains the main administrative, political, cultural, ideological, handicraft and trade center of the region. Both of my father's parents were born in Baku, Azerbaijan.

"Azerbaijan" came from an influence on the local Caucasians with Persian, Median and Turkic tribes, language and cultures. The Turkic tribes arrived in small bands, which led to conquest and Turkification the local population. Over several hundreds of years, the native population adopted the Oghuz language and converted to Islam.

Throughout their ancient past and into modern history, Armenians have experienced religious persecution, genocide and have been forced out of their historic land. The Armenian people have preserved their alphabet, language, culture and Christian faith throughout emperor rule, conquest, and the Soviet Union. The territory and people of the country today known as "Azerbaijan" was then still in Iranian hands until they were occupied by Russia. Under the Treaty of Turkmenchay, Qajar Iran recognized Russian sovereignty over the Erivan Khanate, the Nakhchivan Khanate and the remainder of the Lankaran Khanate, comprising the last parts of the soil of the modern day Azerbaijan Republic.

During the Soviet Union rule, Armenians lived in the Soviet-Armenian Republic, Nagorno Karabakh and Soviet Republic of Azerbaijan. Although the religious minority, Armenians lived and established their roots and heritage in the multi-ethnic, metropolitan, coastal capital of Baku. History and borders evolved around us with changing Armenian, Persian, Assyrian Empires, Kings and Kingdoms, Baku was our home. We were proud to be Bakintsi (what people from Baku called,) and Kavkazsti (people of the Caucasus Mountain region,) as it had its own, unique identity, its own local culture, personality flair, dialect and proud spirit. The ancient Armenian people of the Caucasus Mountains were courageous warriors and freedom fighters with deeply rooted ancestry in biblical and human history.

Both, my paternal grandfather Sarkis Babayan, Բաբայան and grandmother Gohar were born in Baku. Gohar's father, Arshak Gyanzhuntsev, was a Bolshevik. My grandfather was a local political leader and partisan with the Communist Party. When Hitler set his troops heading towards the oil in Baku, my grandfather knew his duty. Volunteering to serve past his prime age, he enlisted with the Baku-Soviet Battalion during WWII and never came back from the front lines. Sending letters back home, my grandfather told my grandmother to name his unborn son (my Papa) "Martin" (root word from mard, մարդ, meaning human in Armenian.) I have just one image of my grandfather, the one of his POW/MIA memorial photo. My Papa's family lived in extreme poverty and he grew up without a father. To this day he cannot talk about his father without walking out of the room to hide his tears. My father's mother died before I was born.

My Mama's side of the family traced their roots back to Ottoman Turkey and their forced deportation during the 1915 Armenian Genocide. My grandmother Lusya's parents were among the children of the genocide policy and mass deportation of Armenians in Ottoman Turkey. My great-grandparents survived the "Trail of Tears" death marches through the Syrian Desert. They were separated from their family and escaped to Cyprus. Eventually her grandparents migrated to Central Asia, working and settling as merchants in Uzbekistan.

My grandmother Lusya was born in Samarkand, Uzbekistan. After the sudden death of her mother, her father remarried and migrated to Baku. Her father, Avanes Badalov, was a shoemaker and a merchant. Her mother, Varsenik, was a homemaker. My Grandfather Rachik's grandfather was a monk in the Armenian Orthodox Church and that is how we inherited the 'Ter' (meaning) 'Saint' in our family surname Ter-Simonyan, Տէր-Սիմոնյան. His father, Baxshi, worked in the Baku oil industry. For his contributions during WWII, Baxshi was decorated and honored as a veteran by the Soviet government. My grandfather's mother, Aza, died when he was a young boy. My grandparents met at the age of 15, at the shop her father patronized and where my grandfather worked as a shoe maker. They soon married and started their family life together. I was fortunate to know my maternal grandparents.

  My grandmother told us about the 1915 Armenian Genocide her grandparents and parents survived, all the family members they saw executed and starved to death. It felt unreal hearing these horror stories of genocide, distant from our peaceful lives in Baku. Sharing the stories of her family's escape to Cyprus, she spoke of witnessed tortures, the drowning of women and children, the stealing of Armenian girls and the barbaric atrocities they witnessed. "Our ancestors live in our veins," she would tell us, tracing the veins on my hands, "just as I live in your veins." For five generations, the common theme in my family was genocide, ethnic killings, dislocation and constant uprooting. This is the Armenian fate.

  Grandmother Lusya would explain to us how Armenians used to be fair skinned and light eyed people, but throughout history, including in 1915, rape was a tool of genocide. Our ancestors had fair skin and lighter eyes, but now we have darker eyes, hair and skin tones. As the darkest child in our family, I was reminded of this every summer playing in the sun. My black hair and features always reminded me of the genocide, even before I knew about it, I could feel it.

> "On my face the evidence of their suffering and their survival. I often feel this pain and shame in looking in the mirror, I feel my ancestors, and cannot escape this generational connection. This explains why Armenian women try everything to lighten their skin, using bleach creams was popular in my family. I used my Mama's bleach cream today, I want to be beautiful too." (Journal entry - age 14)

Grandmother Lusya came from a very musically talented family. She was awarded medals in the Soviet Union as a talented singer. By trade she was a skilled seamstress. From the age of 15, and in her later years, she managed her own tailor shop. Her father used her older sister's birth certificate so she could be hired at a local tailor shop, and she worked there all her life in Baku. Later she brought my Mama into the family business to work as the accountant to keep books in order, process inventory, deliveries and distribution.

My grandparents met in their teens and were married at age 17. My grandmother gave birth to three children; my aunt Jazmen, my Mama, Tamara and my Keri, (uncle, Mama's brother in Armenian) Sergey. She raised them all and disciplined them to be respectable and educated citizens.

My grandmother and her daughters always had the sharpest clothes, which they would design and tailor themselves. Their style was progressive and European influenced. Even in a traditionally modest society, they created cutting edge pieces for their clients and friends. My grandmother was a trend setter and her daughters reflected the same taste and passion for dressing.

It was soon after my Mama began working that she met my father. First, he would just stop in for business to distribute and deliver textiles to their tailor shop, then to see and interact with my Mama. I can never get a straight answer from them about if they dated or if my father proposed to my Mama. I guess part of it is that they come from a time when these things were not talked about, perhaps the other part of it is that maybe my father did not act according to tradition. I do not know. I just know he would not leave her alone.

My grandparents did not approve of him at first, because he was older and because of the line of work he was in. I know that my father's mother was ill and he was taking care of her during this time. She was a diabetic and was bedridden. From my asking and gathering bits and pieces of how they ended up married, I discovered that my father went into my Mama's parents' house one day and said "Pack her things, next Saturday I am marrying your daughter." My grandmother Gohar passed away and my parents didn't have a traditional wedding due to our 40-day mourning period. Soon my brother Aram was born and then I was born.

*My Papa, my Mama, and my brother, Aram
(Baku, 1986)*

*My Mama, my Grandmother and my brother & I
(Baku, 1985)*

My Aunt Lola, Uncle Sergey, Papa, Mama, Grandfather Rachick, Aram, and Grandmother Lusya (Baku, 1986)

*Grandmother Lusya and Grandfather Rachick
(Baku, 1988)*

4

Life in Baku

"My home. This not my home. My home is Baku. My bed is Baku. My toys is Baku. We go everywhere. My home is not everywhere."

(journal entry - age 10)

I remember our home. Our home address is Prospect Lenin Building #154, 12th Floor, Apartment #78. Our home phone number is 62-30-32. This is my home. I miss our home in Baku. I remember how we lived. How my brother and I played, running around the living room and playing with toys in the bedroom. Our parents hosted dinner parties every week it seemed, and set tables starting from the living room into the bedroom to seat all our extended family and guests. We had a beautiful home. My father had his library of books and my Mama her displayed fine dishes and crystal. We had everything we needed. That is how I remember our home. How we live now is not how we used to live.

Our life was perfect in Baku, as perfect as our life could be in a communist society. Our basic needs were met and our quality of life included leisure, luxuries, family time, country homes, rest and long summer holidays. The freedoms we did not know, we could not miss. Life in the Soviet Union was one of every basic needs and decent living conditions provided by the government. My family was well off, above the average living standards of most families. We had a contemporarily furnished home in a new, 16-floor condominium on the 12th floor. From our balcony we could see the large statue of Karl Marx and the city skyline. We had everything we needed to live comfortably and extra. We had a new car, any car was a luxury back then.

My grandparents, relatives, cousins all lived near us. We would have family get-togethers on a weekly basis. We spent summer days on the beach or away in country homes (dacha дача in Russian) with our friends. Most people came to tour, visit Baku and experience it's luxuries. We called it home. People ate caviar as a delicacy, in Baku we called it breakfast. My family had everything we needed to live a good life. Most of all, we had our relatives, our heritage, our culture and our community. If we didn't have what we needed, we had the connections or knew someone who could take care of things. There was never a feeling of lack in our home. This was our standard of living.

Our doors could stay open and often did to welcome friends and family, or simply for us to play out in the main corridor. My parents never taught us to see the differences in people. They had Russian friends, Jewish friends, Muslim friends, and there was never a talk of us and them. I remember an old family friend who was Muslim bringing us sweets and candy whenever she was visiting our home. Our family doctors, teachers, and my parents' work colleagues were Muslims, Jews and Christians. They impressed upon us the importance of being people of good character, people of ethics and honor. That was the only difference we were to distinguish among people, their character, their honor and their word. My father and mother were conscious of the way they raised us.

Growing up, I heard my parents share about their life in Baku. Before identity politics, people of different ethnic backgrounds lived peacefully together during in the Soviet Union. The Armenian community was vibrant in Baku, with over 300,000 ethnic Armenians calling it home.

During Soviet rule, everyone's first identity was as Soviet Citizens. However, as ethnic Armenians we continued to keep our language, religion, culture and traditions alive.

From a very young age children were indoctrinated to perform civic duties bettering the Soviet Union and pushing forward the Communist principles. My brother and I wore uniforms and learned songs in our government daycare and school programs. Communism saturated every institution of our society. Not everyone was a communist or followed the communist ideology. My family was not partisan or affiliated with the local Parties. It was a mandatory requirement for government workers, law enforcement, court clerks, state officials and administrators to join the Party. Those who were faithful to the Party ideology lived simple and humble lives. Those at the top, like in any form of government, lined their own pockets. Ordinary people who desired a better life, and had the spirit of an entrepreneur, made their own way.

Corruption and bribery were a lifeline in the Soviet Union. The 'Black Market', or counter economy in the Soviet Union, was much stronger and vibrant than the government controlled economy. My father was a Soviet counter-economy entrepreneur. Speculation was common practice in the Soviet Union, most everyone knew if they couldn't get something in the stores, most likely they knew someone who knew someone who could get it in the "shadow economy." Any opportunity to hustle, flip goods and turn profit, his tight knit circle of black-marketeers was in on it. They understood free market economics better than the minister of economy in Baku. They knew the fundamentals of supply and demand and how to flip government distributed inventory for personal profit. Simple economics.

Financially we were secure, we never worried about money. My father worked his way out of poverty, educated by the streets. My Mama worked but did not need to work. She worked with her mother at the atelier, making the salary of an accountant. My father made really good money. This is not to brag, there is no way to brag about this. We could not live flashy lives, nobody could. Making that sort of money back home was dangerous. Even if you could afford something fancy, you would bring too much attention to yourself. Here is the difference between our life in the Soviet Union and in America. In the Soviet Union we could make lots of money but there was nothing to buy! In America, we make very little money and there is everything one can imagine to buy!

*My Mama and Papa
(Baku, 1981)*

*My Father's home library
(Baku, 1984)*

My Aunt Jazmen holding me, my Grandfather Rachick, my cousin Armine, my brother Aram, my Father and my Mama (Baku, March 1984)

*My Grandfather and Father grilling shish kebab on the 12th floor balcony of our home
(Baku, March 1984)*

5

Becoming Refugees

"War kills childhood, everything else can be rebuilt."

(journal entry - age 11)

Our whole life turned into a horrific nightmare after the most praised moment of modern history. "Mr. Gorbachev tear down this wall." While the world celebrated the fall of Berlin Wall in 1989, we on the other side of the wall were beginning to feel the rumbling of identity politics. The Soviet Union was crumbling, and with it our Soviet identity, security, stability and entire life. Maybe the West played a role in the fall of the Soviet super power. Maybe it was Gorbachev's Glasnost, or 'openness' that gave way to the domino effect that led to ethnic clash. Maybe the people were simply fed up with oppression and suffocation by ideology. It wasn't well thought out, the breaking down of an empire and all the people on the other side of that Wall. The different politics intersected, creating the energy and space for identity movements to erupt throughout the crumbling Soviet Union.

Nationalism was spreading through the USSR, former republics declaring their independence. This was the beginning of the fall of communism in Azerbaijan. Armenians living in Azerbaijan were suddenly targeted, harassed, and attacked in the streets in Baku. Extreme nationalism and anti-Armenian sentiment took over the radio, media and political climate in Azerbaijan in the fall of the Soviet Empire. The ethnic cleansing campaign was in direct retaliation against the demands of Nagorno-Karabakh Armenians to secede from Azerbaijan. My parents, like many Armenians, could not imagine the living nightmare that would occur next. At least you can wake up from a nightmare, this real-life horror we could not wake up from.

"The fish stinks from the head." The phrase I heard most repeated over and over again by my grandparents when talking about the ethnic killings in Baku following the collapse of the Soviet Union. It is a common phrase pointing out that most political problems and social conflict come from the heads of government. Ethnic killings of Armenians began on February 27, 1988, in the city of Sumgait, just 18 miles away from the capital Baku, where we lived.

Following Sumgait, demonstrations and rallies were organized in Baku, the men were given address lists of Armenian neighborhoods, homes and places of employment. Armenian homes were identified and marked with a cross on a map of the city. Immediately my family went into hiding. The persecution and hate crimes against Armenian civilians intensified in Baku.

The massacre of Armenians was organized by top officials of Azerbaijan. Overnight, leaders changed the tone on the news, radio programs and spoke of a movement of identity politics, nationalism and an Azerbaijan free of Armenians. The people were emboldened by the opportunistic Popular Front of Azerbaijan (PFA) leadership who fueled "us and them' sentiment to further their political agenda. These leaders organized demonstrations throughout the city capitol attracting tens and thousands of men.

Gorbachev sent in Soviet troops and Martial Law was declared in Baku, but this was a temporary calm. Demonstration crowds grew, emboldened by the anti-Armenian rhetoric. The crowds were supplied with iron rods, steel pipes and knives. The men were wearing matching trench coats! They had addresses of Armenian homes. How did they get so organized?

> *"To blame religion is unfair and does not correctly place responsibility where it belongs. I do not blame religion. I blame politicians. I hear some say "people are sheep,' but that is an insult to the sheep. Sheep don't organize mass killings and slaughter one another." (Journal entry - age 14)*

Regardless of one's ethnicity, culture, religion, or the institutions we are born into, which groom us to learn, to obey and to follow - very few of us stop to question the creeping force of "us and them" divisive politics. As we learn from history, the few who do are often punished, imprisoned, or even worse, killed. In Azerbaijan, officials camouflaged their planned massacre of Armenians with rhetoric language of national identity, independence and self-determination of Azerbaijan, using their own people to commit crimes against humanity. The Azerbaijani people were brainwashed into the cruelty of hunting, attacking and killing their Armenian neighbors and friends. "People are sheep," I heard someone say once. This is an insult to the sheep, sheep do not organize to exterminate other sheep. Only humans are capable of such deep evil as genocide.

We lived on the 12th floor. From the balcony, I saw the rallies, large crowds of tens and thousands of men marching during the demonstrations. They looked like ants. For a child, it was a bird's eye view of hell to see humanity come to a point of such hate, so much as to hunt and kill people. There is no way to explain how primitive this fear feels – the fear of being hunted. The tension could be felt leading up to the actual violence, but no one could imagine that it would actually happen. It happened so fast that many of the Armenians became trapped in their own homes, unable to leave the country.

Some Armenians believed that things would settle down, and things would go back to normal. It would be safe again for Armenians to live in Baku. The majority didn't take their chances and left quickly. Over 300,000 Baku Armenians fled into neighboring countries as refugees. Those that could made arrangements to switch homes with Azeri families in neighboring Georgia, Russia or Armenia. In our own family there was division on staying or leaving. Our father did not hesitate; he knew history too well to be optimistic about our safety.

My parents first put my brother and I on the last bus leaving Baku in October 1988, we didn't know if we would see each other again. The Spitak (Armenian City) earthquake occurred on December 7, 1988 with a magnitude of 6.8, devastating Armenia in middle of a refugee humanitarian crisis. Our family went from surviving ethnic killings, to again becoming refugees, this time environmental refugees in the Armenian earthquake. The despair in Armenia from local and arriving refugees trying to survive a winter without electricity, water, shelter, kerosene or food, was worse than in war. I went back to Baku a couple times after that. The last time I was in Baku was in late October 1989, with my parents to gather documents.

Armenian newspaper interview of our refugee family at the airplane crash site following the earthquake of December 1988. My cousin, Sarkis Babayan, was a soldier among the deceased aboard this plane delivering humanitarian aid.

Fleeing from Baku via train, arriving in Yerevan, Armenia (May 1989)

My brother, Aram, embraces my Mama for the first time since we were separated.
(Yerevan, May 1989)

6

Baku Pogroms

"Every time I brush my teeth I remember her, I see her. My flashbacks and nightmares begin and end with Lola."

(journal entry - age 15)

The pogroms in Baku reached their peak in January 1990. From January 12, a seven-day pogrom broke out against the Armenian civilian population. Thousands did not escape and fell victim to the organized mobs rioting, torturing, raping, dismembering and killing of Armenian men, women, the elderly and children. The mobs were prepared with maps of Armenian neighborhoods and communicated with each other using hand held radios. The phone lines in the Armenian neighborhoods were cut and Armenians were instructed to stay home by their employers. The anti-Armenian pogroms lasted seven days until the Soviet Troops were deployed into the city. To be an Armenian in January 1990 in Baku was a death sentence. This ethnic genocide in Baku of Armenians is known as Black January.

Relatives and neighbors could be heard screaming for help as they were beaten, robbed, and raped during the Baku pogroms in January. Women were stripped and forced to dance naked in the streets then, beaten or killed. Women in the maternity hospital were attacked, stabbed and their unborn ripped out of their wombs and killed. Out in the open streets, bystanders and police watched Armenians being dismembered, beaten and set on fire alive. They watched as their remains were mutilated. Mass-distributed iron rods, knives and axes were used to break into homes in order to beat and kill Armenians. This was done without mercy for babies, children or the elderly. Our departed loved ones were not left without violence, their tombstones were vandalized, defaced and destroyed in the Baku Armenian cemetery. Whose religion allows this dishonor?

My aunt Lola was working for a military office and was living at our grandparent's apartment of the eighth floor. My grandparent's address was Rosa Luxemburg #19, 8th floor, home #21. Their house was packed; my grandmother was making arrangements to ship their belongings. My grandfather was on work assignment providing humanitarian aid to the Earthquake victims in Armenia. My uncle was stuck in St. Petersburg; no planes or trains were traveling to Baku due to the reported pogroms.

On January 13th, the mobs were sweeping through the neighborhoods looking for apartments and homes marked previously with crosses, symbolizing where Christian Armenians lived. If anyone called the police, if their phone was on, the dispatch would say the police are on their way. The police would never show up, instead the mobs of men were tipped off where Armenians were calling in from. The mob entered my grandparent's apartment complex, dragged and beat an Armenian man to death who lived a few floors above my grandparent's floor. On January 11th, my Mama spoke to my aunt Lola, my uncle's wife, who was staying at my grandparent's home, with concern about the dangers of increasing anti-Armenian violence in Baku. Lola said she was not going in to work, that she was told to stay home. This was the last time we would hear from her.

The day we found out about what happened to Lola seems so unreal, even after all these years. It replays in my mind. No matter how hard I try not to think about it, her death still haunts me. How could someone do such a thing? Commit such a hateful and inhumane crime against a young woman, a new mother, someone's daughter, someone's wife and innocent human. I first heard my uncle Abo, my Mama's sister's husband, say that Lola has been killed when he came home from work. He had to sit down because he could not handle even uttering the words to the rest of the family.

My aunt Lola was home alone when she heard the mob of men outside her door. The men broke down the door into the apartment as the neighbors just watched and no one did anything to intervene. As she screamed from the eighth floor for help, they tortured, raped and beat her. Then, while she was still alive, they threw her out of the eighth floor balcony into the streets. They left her to suffer and hold on to whatever little life that was still in her. Out of everyone in the street, and in the apartment complex, no one called for help or gave her medical assistance.

Some official documents stated cause of death as "head trauma, bleeding" while other documents fabricated dates and egregiously listed "natural cause of death" as the manner in which her life was removed from her. However, witnesses gave full detail about the brutal torture, rape, and beatings of her and other Armenians in the building. The Azerbaijan government falsified death certificates, spreading the dates of the deceased during the Baku pogroms. They wanted to hide any evidence of concentrated numbers of mass murders and ethnic killings taking place in Baku during that week.

My grandmother, under a fake Russian name and passport, was escorted back to Baku, to her house after the January pogroms. She entered the house and saw with her eyes where the violence had taken place. With the help of the KGB, she acquired official government documents, accounting the injuries, and the evidence of the torture our aunt Lola suffered and died from. The KGB investigator issued a document, noting the beatings, bruises on her legs, cigarette burns and markings on her body, and extreme impact to her skull from being thrown off the 8th floor balcony.

The Azerbaijan government would not allow our family to take her body. Her work colleagues assured our family that they gave her a proper burial, but we will never know. My uncle's heart was forever left with an open wound after losing the love of his life. My cousin Elona was left motherless. Our aunt was murdered in cold blood. Our family was left without closure and without the honorable burial our culture demands for our loved ones. The Azerbaijani government got away with these crimes against humanity. With Armenian blood on their guilty hands, they shake the hands of world leaders today.

The beatings, robberies, tortures, rapes and murders in Baku terrorized our human wholeness, psychologically, mentally, and spiritually. The terrorism we experienced, physically left us homeless and emotionally deformed. As children it killed our childhood, traumatizing us into our adulthood. It traumatized our parents, grandparents, our entire family. No one person in my family was unaffected by the violent pogroms in Baku. Our family stories are exchanges of sadness, loss and despair. We used to be very humorous and happy - a very happy family. Now, the sadness overshadows any happiness. We are just one family, there are tens of thousands of Armenian families from Azerbaijan with murdered family members.

Before, memories of my Aunt Lola were full of joy. Her kindness and beauty drew me to her as a little girl. Her soft spoken grace and easy going personality was pleasant to me. She taught me how to brush my teeth as a child, cupping my hand to bring water to my mouth. Every time I brush my teeth I remember her, I see her. Reliving this simple memory brings back the horror that took her away from our family. My flashbacks and nightmares begin and end with Lola. The triggers are as simple as a toothbrush; the memories feel just as real as when they happened. I cannot get rid of these thoughts and images repeating in my head.

We experienced the worst human evil possible at such a young age. We were robbed of normal parent-child memories that are sweet, safe and secure. We were children in the middle of this hell. All I wanted was to be a child. I wanted to have my parents, not their trauma, to raise me. Now our family is wounded. My family is not well. We are all wounded, emotionally hollow, permanently scattered, fragmented and stuck in our family trauma. We are all dead inside, even if we are alive still. We will not have closure until we have justice.

In Loving Memory of Lolita (Mikaelyan) Ter-Simonyan

My Uncle Sergey with my Aunt Lola and cousin, Elona (Baku, New Year's 1986)

My Uncle Sergey and my Grandfather Rachick, in accordance with Armenian tradition, grow out their facial hair during the 40 days of mourning my Aunt Lola
(1990)

7

Homeless

"Pretending to be anywhere else than where I was, anything else than who I was...I learned to disappear."

(journal entry - age 13)

First, we were refugees fleeing ethnic killings. Now, in Armenia, we again became refugees but this time due to natural disaster. I was playing on my aunt's balcony when the high rise building began to shake. Standing on the balcony and moving with the building was very confusing to me, I didn't know what was happening. After a few minutes, again and again the building shook. Watching from the balcony I saw my brother running from the school towards the apartment. We all ran outside and stood in the streets. This was the first time I heard about earthquakes. We were scared to go inside that night afraid of the aftershocks.

With the burden of fleeing refugees and the most catastrophic earthquake to hit the second largest city of Spitak, Armenia was at the complete mercy of the international community. The second largest city in Armenia was wiped out entirely. The Soviet leaders hesitated to allow journalists and humanitarian response aid in, fearing they would also see the fleeing refugees from the pogroms in Baku. They waited as long as they could. Local Armenians were already struggling to survive the crumbling Soviet economy; now, Armenian refugees fleeing from Azerbaijan added to the humanitarian crisis.

Meanwhile, in Azerbaijan, people danced in the streets celebrating the Earthquake in Armenia. In Armenia, we mourned and held mass funerals for 25,000 men, women, and children. Humanitarian aid could not reach Armenia with threats from Azerbaijan to shoot planes down. The nuclear plant was shut down in fear of aftershocks following the earthquake. I remember the way it felt, the deep grief and sadness on the faces of adults. I felt as if God turned his face away from Armenia.

Everyone was trying to survive; the whole country came to a standstill. There was no work. No shelter. No power or electricity. No food. No gasoline. Nothing. Absolutely nothing. We might as well have stayed in Baku; our chances were just as equal surviving there as it was for us now in Armenia. Homeless, and without income, our family's future was bleak.

By coincidence, my father met a man who was the principal of local school in a small town outside of the capital Yerevan, town called Yeghvard. After hearing about our escape from Baku and homeless circumstance, he showed my father a small utility storage for broken school equipment. My father without hesitation, took the offer to clean up the space and provide us with some shelter.

My father decided to sleep in his car in the dead of winter to save on the drive back and forth from the capital where we stayed. During the day, in the freezing weather, he gathered the scraps of material he found to clean and patch up holes in the ground where the rats made nests. These were no ordinary rats, during a time when people were starving, the rats in Armenia were the size of medium sized lap dogs, aggressive and also starving.

With whatever skills he had, he drew a pipe from a local school plumbing system to provide us with water for boiling and cooking, and a kerosene stove for heat and cooking. When we moved in, although the spot was hidden, inside it looked like a small studio created out of mismatched material. How he transformed the space was amazing. It was ugly but it was ours. Even more important, we were together, and, for now, safe.

We had nothing, just a few personal belongings, blankets and things my parents brought to Armenia. Every day we struggled to stay alive. I would eat whatever I could find outside. My parents did their best to provide for us, but there was simply nothing to buy in the grocery stores. People were starving, freezing to death.

I hated living. I hated being a child. I hated people. My first day of school was the most humiliating day of my life, I walked out of the storage and all the children saw me going to class.

My only happiness came from sharing the days wandering around the courtyard with my brother, getting lost in my imagination. Pretending to be anywhere else then where I was, anyone other than who I was. I learned to disappear. We survived in this storage without electricity, water or bathrooms while we waited to be vetted for our refugee status.

So much of our identity is attached to a space, our shelter we grow to feel comfort and safety in. The feeling of having no space of your own, or being robbed of your security and shelter shatters your sense of self and confidence. It is a real, physical feeling of hollowness. An emotional fear and emptiness that nothing else can compare to. Being homeless brought me shame and sadness daily.

Whether poor or average, it seemed that everyone else had a respectable home to live in, while my family cohabitated with rats in a school's storage. My parents did their best to pretend it was home and convince us it was okay but the feeling of shame and dehumanizing conditions reminded us that it was not.

I remember living those years with my spirit heavy with sadness, and my head lowered so as to not be noticed or asked by anyone who I was or where I lived. I was scared to be mocked at school or beaten up for being so poor. When I was homeless, I learned to feel nothing. I rejected my emotions to ignore the reality of our desperate life. Being alive felt so disgusting to me. I would pretend I was someone else to escape in my mind.

My first day of school was filled with some of the most humiliating moments of my life. At age seven, I hated my life because it felt like a never ending punishment. The children made fun of me for not knowing Armenian. I was embarrassed by our obvious poverty. I remember praying to the icons my Mama had on the wall, praying for a home. Praying almost every day, that God would get us out of this rat nest, and would make it so we were not living in such a disgusting space.

It was so filthy, even after my Mama scrubbed every inch of the place, dirty and infested with rat droppings. One door lead in from the outside courtyard and the other lead out into the main hallway into the school building. We had no bathroom in our storage, and the school's restrooms were out of service, and full of rats. People still used the broken bathrooms, it was the most disgusting stench through the school.

We were so scared to walk the hall or go to the restrooms because the rats would attack or jump on us. We resorted to using a pan to go to the bathroom, and taking it to the canal to dispose of. For us this was very dirty and a violation of our dignity, but there was no other choice.

I felt like an animal, disgusting and exposed going to the bathroom like that. I would hold it as long as I could, afraid to go to the bathroom. Some other people would just go on the streets, or on the school yard ground, which made it so unhealthy and disgusting to live around. Eventually we became numb to this dehumanizing condition and did not speak about it much, just knew it was our only choice.

I was so ashamed to be alive. I did not feel like a human child, I felt like an animal. The rats would play in the human waste and then run around the building, touching all surfaces of the school. This was a functional school, and daily the children would attend and be exposed to such gross factors, there was not much anyone could do about.

Our storage had two beds, one for my parents and one for my brother and I. There was a small cooking area with a sink, shelf, kerosene stove that was also used to provide heat to the room, and a small TV that never seemed to work, unless one of us held the antenna the whole time. We had a wooden bench and a chair and table, we always ate at the table.

My Mama had her small vanity, dresser and linen drawer, and that was all we owned. The room was lined with recycled pieces of rugs on the floor. There was a small window in the room covered in metal bars. The room was cold, so my father put up several electric heaters to keep us warm at night, sometimes they would work if we had electricity, but mostly we lived in the dark with candles and kerosene to keep us warm.

The cold in Armenia, especially during those winters, was so harsh. It was painful to sleep at night. Your body ached from how long it shivered and the muscles tensed up. Nights especially were unfortunate for us, since we did not always have electricity or available kerosene to burn, shivering and clicking our teeth until we all fell asleep.

In the mornings, my Mama would give us a cup of tea and maybe a piece of bread and send us off to school. Each morning was the same shameful walk to our class. I remember looking around quickly before walking out of the storage into the hallway, afraid someone would see us and make fun of us, or tell on us that we were staying in the school. It was a constant feeling of fear and humiliation. My anxiety and dislike for learning developed very young.

I would run quickly to my classroom, knowing that punishment was served for tardiness and disturbing class after the bell rang. My brother went to class down the hall from me, he was in a grade higher than I, and we would not see each other all day. This separation made it even harder for us to defend each other from the bullies and fights from the mean children, who knew of our poverty and misfortunate homelessness. I hated going to school. As well as I did, I still hated going and being treated like trash every day.

My parents did their very best to keep us clean and respectable looking when sending us off to school, but we did not always have the right color uniform or supplies, and the children made sure we were aware of just how unwelcome we were. The teacher humiliated me in front of my class when I did not have the right uniform or hair bows on picture day. I was forced to change my bows and borrow some from a classmate. At recess, the older kids isolated us and threw rocks at us, threatening to kill our parents.

We did not speak fluent Armenian, because in Baku we spoke Russian and, in Armenia, the Russian language was frowned upon so we were mocked for our funny accents. I tried to ignore the harassment, the name calling, the threats and the hitting. Everyday children would tell us to go back to where we came from, or spit on us for being refugees from Baku. These were our own people treating us with such hate. I did not understand; I still cannot understand how this much hate could be in small children.

It was a daily battle and one the teachers could care less to resolve; they were concerned with teaching with the limited resources they had. The teachers too showed prejudice towards my brother and I. I remember being punished in front of the class for having a little dirt under my fingernails. We did not have running water for days and I had no way to wash my hands. The teacher beat my hands with her wooden ruler as the children watched me cry.

One day a girl stole the teachers color pencils and put them inside my backpack. I did not know that she put them inside my backpack when I was outside. When the teacher searched everyone's bags and found them in mine, she screamed at me calling me a refugee thief and spanked me in front of everyone! I cried and told the teacher I didn't take her pencils, but she didn't believe me because I was the poorest child in class. She assumed because we were poor and homeless, that we were also thieves. I hated school so much, even though we lived in it, I wished a bomb would fall on it.

Lunch time proved to us our real poverty. As all the other children ate pea soup and xachapuri խաչապուրի (cheese stuffed bread,) we just watched and enjoyed the aroma. My mouth would water thinking of what it must have tasted like to eat those warm, stuffed rolls. I wished someone would offer me a taste of the soup, just once. I was hungry all the time. Even now, in America, I eat as much as I can, even when I am full. When I would finish with my food at school here, I would eat my friend's leftovers. If I'm at my friend's house, I'll eat as much as I can.

When we were homeless in Armenia, my brother and I would find leftover chunks and crumbs in the cafeteria after everyone ate, or after school and would eat them. Finding those crumbs made me so happy. I would eat food off the floor, off the streets, whatever I found or could clean off enough to feed myself. Sometimes I would find a half-eaten corn cob, candy or some treat to eat and share it with my brother.

    I learned I could eat just about anything that grew in nature, and I did. My parents did not know about my foraging habits, they provided food best they could. We ate dinner together, but not much and during the day there was no one home to eat lunch so we became little hunters and gatherers around our school yard and streets. We never let our parents know we did this, because it would upset them. I remember feeling guilty for eating, even though we had very little food ourselves. To snack between meals, I would mix water and flower and cook little flat breads for my brother and I. In the spring we gathered fruit and ate small flowers that were sweet with nectar, grass and plants with salt too.

    During the day, my Mama worked at a fur factory, sewing together bits of rabbit fur to make small clothing items and slippers. It paid very little. Her tailor skills helped in finding some employment at a factory with my Aunt and cousin. They worked long hours and were paid very little. My father found employment at a local mechanic shop, but the collapsing Soviet government and economy left him without pay for months. Like most Armenian men, my father could fix anything. Cars were his area of expertise, and he understood most machines. There was very little work requested by the public. People did not need their cars fixed, most people couldn't even afford gasoline to run their cars. Distribution trucks did not need to be serviced since there were no goods to be distributed.

He soon became an assistant manager, which still paid him in 'I-Owe-You's.' the position was good for the small privileges it presented. Lucky for my father, his shop had kerosene and he rationed some to use for cooking and heat. This kept us from freezing to death. We were not unique in our struggle to survive, only unique in how we were surviving. The entire country was devastated. The people had no progress, nowhere to work, nothing to buy, no food to eat and very little hope left. This was Armenia post-Soviet Union collapse. This was our form of existence for three long and cold years.

I don't know how my parents did it. How did they manage to keep us alive with no heat or food? How did they keep our life going? How did they keep up their hope, faith and moral strength? Most married people, most individuals, would fall into despair from the helplessness and the conditions my parents faced. Their courage and endurance fascinates me to this day. Did they cry in private I wonder? I used to listen at night, I never heard or saw their tears. They managed to keep us alive day after day, keeping us fed, sheltered, and safe from the cold. It was getting more and more difficult towards the end of our third year.

My Mama did not work because she broke her hand. My father's job was still not paying for the hours he worked. They sold most of their belongings and we were going through our canned food very quickly. Winter was getting near and there was no more access to kerosene or electricity available to keep heaters working. Food rations were handed out but there was very little food to distribute. People were starving. Animals were starving because there were simply no scraps left in the streets for them.

My brother and I walked for miles, stood in line and waited for bread to be distributed. Hungry people who didn't have rations watched us stand in line wanting our loaf. Grown men, starving, sometimes stole bread from the little children. It was a team effort huddling the loaf with my brother to make sure to get it back home. The older boys in the neighborhood routinely attacked and fought with us, taking whatever we had, threatening to rape me or my Mama, scaring my brother. I carried a large stick in case we were attacked, or if someone tried to steal our bread from us. I was ready to stab, beat and even kill for our own protection. I told my brother to hold it tucked under his jacket and tight with his hands. We had to survive, we had to eat. It was so tempting to bite into that fresh warm bread, our little mouths would water.

As much as I was afraid of disappointing my parents if anything happened, I was more afraid of not having bread for our family to eat that night. It didn't matter how much money you had, there was nothing to buy in the stores! There was no gasoline. People were stealing gasoline out of each other's car tanks. You could be in line for gasoline for three hours and by the time it was your turn there was no more for your car. I don't understand why we had rations when the grocery stores were empty, pointless when there is no food to ration.

One day the grocery store was completely empty except for the large pile of cabbage. The whole store was empty; it was as if you could hear echoes from people whispering. I thought to myself, "Who needs that much cabbage?" My Mama bought all the cabbage she and I could carry and pickled it in large buckets. I asked her, "What?! Are we going to eat pickled tomatoes and cabbage all winter??" She answered, "We will eat what God provides us, be grateful, some people have less than us."

My Aunt Jazmen standing outside the school storage which was our shelter for nearly 4 years.
(Yegvard, 2000)

8

God Provided

"My best memory with my brother is the day we made a sled from a metal back off an old T.V. We piled the snow to be 5 feet tall and took turns sliding down in the metal container. I carved steps in the slope for us to climb up. We laughed so much that day."

(journal entry - age 13)

Somehow God provided. Somehow we survived each day. Some days it was a stranger who saw us living in the school and brought fruit to us. Some days my father found an opportunity to earn some money. Some days my dad's friends, also struggling to eat, would invite us over to share a meal. Other times, it was simply a miracle.

One Spring afternoon, I was playing in the school courtyard as usual. Our mother would not let us leave the court yard or go past the fence. There were three brick walls from the school and the court yard was all paved with no grass or flowers, just asphalt and bricks. I was playing with some mud when I noticed small plants growing near the sewer line. The plants were about 4-inches with interesting leaves on them that caught my attention. I remembered at my uncle's farm seeing these same leaves when he was teaching me about farming. If I remembered right, these were tomato plants. I showed them to my brother, but he didn't know what they were.

I started to shovel some dirt with a bowl and brought nice clean dirt to a pile next to our storage home steps. After I made a large pile of dirt, I carefully uprooted the plants next to our door. Just then, an old woman walked by the fence. When she was close enough, I waved at her to get her attention. I showed her the small plants and asked if she thought they were tomatoes. She said no, but may God bless them and make them provide me with an abundance of tomatoes.

I took care of those plants every day. I dug a small pathway for water to get to them from the canal. I put sticks next to the stem to protect them from breaking. My father shook his head saying that they were never going to grow because they were on top of asphalt. Months passed and the plants got bigger. Two out of four plants survived and grew taller. I kept giving them water and making sure there were no bugs on them or weeds growing next to them, just like my uncle taught me.

One morning I went outside to play, and there were small yellow flowers on the plants. I was so happy! I haven't felt this happy in a long time. I ran inside and told my Mama that I was sure they were tomato plants and that we were going to have fresh tomatoes soon! She was encouraging and told me to keep up the good work caring for them. After a few good sunny months, we grew enough tomatoes for my Mama to can, pickle and share, an abundance of tomatoes for sure. God blessed us again.

Growing tomatoes was one of the happiest memory I recall from our homeless years. Those tomatoes gave me purpose, they needed me to survive. Gardening was my little escape from horrible life we were living. I felt attached to the plants, they were my friends. I cared for them, giving them the cleanest water I could find. When it rained I collected water for the plants. When it hailed, I worried they would break. Watching them grow gave me a good feeling.

During the nice weather, my brother and I spent most of our time playing outside. We loved to be outside, inside felt like a prison for rats. Our storage home was a scary box surrounded by huge rats that my father had to fight off with a branch. Outside we could forget our sadness. During the school year, we had to stay inside more so kids wouldn't see us living there. We hated going to school.

Every morning began with a sad reality of the kids making fun of us at school for being homeless and living in the school's storage. Our own peers terrorized us when we were at the lowest point in our life. My brother and I came home from school every day with tears in our eyes from the insults, hits and being spat on. Although we were Armenia, the kids would still terrorize us and call us names for being refugees from Azerbaijan. They called us traitors and Turks to insult us. The adults were worst, harassing and vandalizing our dwelling, smearing feces on our doors. The teachers did very little, perhaps they felt the same as the kids about us, but couldn't express it.

My Mama kept us extremely clean, and our uniforms mended to promote our dignity although we were homeless. Many times we had to wash our heads with kerosene to get rid of lice we got from children at school. We would sit and wait while our heads burned to kill the lice. My mother took time to look through our head every day.

We would cry about how much children harassed us. She emphasized in us our character and manners regardless of how others treated us. She always reminded us that we are people of compassion, consciousness and pride, to keep our heads high. My father would have his extremes, at times it was encouraging us to fight back, other times he would remind us that God sees everything and will judge everyone accordingly.

My brother and I were very lonely kids. We could not have friends because of how we lived. We living in hiding from the rest of our neighbors, suspicious and afraid of everyone. We didn't have toys to help us escape, we pretended and it was good enough. We played with sticks, rocks and mud, building little homes and figures out of them. My best memory with my brother is the day we made a sled from a metal back off an old T.V. We piled up the snow to be 5 feet tall and took turns sliding down in the metal container. I even carved steps in the slope to make it easier for us to climb up. We laughed so much that day, it was the best day we had together living in that school.

During the evenings we sat around the table, reading and watching the candles burn. We did not have lights or any electricity. The heat from the kerosene stove kept us warm some nights. My Mama mended our clothes, my father would be fixing something and my brother and I would recycle the wax from the burning candles. We used string and the melted wax to make new candles by hand. I think that is why I have such a high tolerance for heat; from making candles from hot wax. Watching the candle was calming, it was dark, but the candle showed me all the faces I loved.

We would talk about school. My father talked to us about politics and history, lecture us on how great Armenia used to be, and that Armenians are the first Christians. He would always end his lectures with realizing that we were living the product of our Christian faith, and that our suffering and persecution has been generational. I thought, we must be praying to the wrong God since we are punished so much. He would remind us that we are blessed because we are alive, we have a roof over our head and there are people who are struggling worse than us. My Mama reassured us that school would get better, and encouraged us to learn Armenian.

Both my father and mother were cautious of protecting whatever innocence was left in us and our childhood. They made sure that although we have been exposed to violence and prejudice, that we didn't develop anger towards people. My brother and I wanted to hate something, someone, to make sense of what or who did this to us. We were two children lost in our emotions, confused by the sadness in our hearts. We didn't care who, we just needed to hate something. We were children and we felt the hate of the entire world.

My parents didn't express their private thoughts or prejudices to us. I'm sure they experienced intense depression, anger, frustration and hate. They were careful about how they talked with us and what they would talk to us about. They were conscious of the possible prejudices it would form in us if they expressed their adult opinions to children. They never identified any one group of people as an enemy, not ethnic or religious. It confused us even more that they were so calm about telling us that there are good and bad in every religion and ethnic group.

My Mama and Papa raised us the best they could in an environment of persecution they could not control. They were wise to not allow hate to infect our young hearts. Even when I would ask my father, "why we don't go and kill the people that are killing us?" he would simply say, "Then we would be just like them," and make me think about it. I thought saying hateful things about the people that robbed, tortured, killed and threw us out of our home would make my parents proud, and when it disappointed them, it made me aware of their expectations. Their expectation was for us to be decent, honorable and compassionate children - even if our environment did not reflect these traits back to us.

    I imagine the most difficult task for my parents was not keeping our tummies from hunger, but protecting our spirits from darkness. My parents were not child psychologists, or experts on child development, they were winging parenthood like everyone with love. They knew that all they had of value was the most important value of all, their children's safety, happiness and health. They were not perfect, but they were most perfect at preserving love and compassion in our little hearts. They taught us right and wrong. Our parents made sure we never stole, never took without asking and never hurt any other human being, to not bring dishonor to our family. It was their expectation, homeless or not, for us to be compassionate, kind, respectful and conscious little people.

    It was hard to believe my parents when they spoke of our future and "God willing' better days. It seemed to me that our God abandoned us long ago. I didn't feel any God anywhere around us, just violence, hate and desperation. How could I believe in something, or fear something that was absent throughout all our suffering and pain? I was scared of people trying to kill us more than I was scared of any God. My parents didn't talk openly about their faith. Occasionally, they would remind us of how God punishes those who throw bread away. One night I overheard my father praying while he was sitting and smoking on the steps. He was looking to the stars, and he was whispering. I heard him pray.

"I never ask you for anything. Help us. God don't let me see my children starve. Don't let this family die. We have no more to sell. We are to the bottom of our canned food. The winter is months away. We have no more kerosene. We will freeze to death. God don't let me see my children freeze to death. God don't let me see my wife get sick from the cold. Get us out of here. Send us anywhere. I will do the rest. I will work any job to feed my family. Just get us out of here, so we don't die."

It was not until I heard my Papa pray to God that night that I understood death might be near for us too. That moment scared me back into believing. If my father was praying, it must be serious, there must be a real God. I started to pray for God to answer my father's prayer too. I did not want my family to die.

My grandmother, Aunt Jazmen, Mama, Uncle Abo, cousin and brother and I outside the church where we held my cousin Elona's baptism.
(Yerevan, 1991)

My father and grandfather cooking shish kebab in Moscow, Russia. These are among the last photographs taken before leaving for the United States (August 1992)

*Waiting to leave to the United States
(August 1992)*

My Grandmother along with my cousins, Arman & Elona, and my brother & I (August 1992)

*Elona, Aram, and me
(August 1992)*

9

Coming to America

"As the plane landed, I felt the girl I was in Armenia start to disappear. All of a sudden I did not exist. I don't know who we are in this new land."

(journal entry - age 12)

The day we left Armenia for the United States is forever fresh in my memory. It was the end of summer in 1992, I was nine years old. We rode the train from Armenia to Moscow, living there a few months while waiting for our final refugee vetting and interview. Staying with our grandparents in their temporary refugee housing, it was crowded in one room. After the Baku pogroms, some refugee families were issued rooms in hotels, dormitories and sanatoriums in Russia. My grandparents lost everything when their home was broken into, now they lived in a hotel room in Gulubaya Rechka Голубая Речка (Light Blue River) near a forest, outside of Moscow.

I loved exploring the forest and finding berries, mushrooms and nuts to eat. My cousins were with us there and we would play together. My oldest cousin Arman carved wooden figurines and model churches out of the aspen tree bark. I loved watching him work with his hands. My cousin Armine knit, so I learned by watching her. My cousin Elona and I would wander into the forest and find little animals to catch. We would go as far into the forest as we could to explore and gather nuts before it got dark outside.

Nearby, there was a river where all the visitors would fish and swim. One day I was playing by the water when my brother threw someone's toy into the river. I reached for the toy doll and walked into the river. Quickly the current pulled me in and I started to drown. I remember pushing with my feet to bring myself up, but the water kept covering my head. I waved and tried to scream for my grandfather. I panicked and swallowed the water. The last thing I remember is seeing my grandfather take his pants off to jump in, and a young man in his swimming clothes came running. I woke up on the grass, crying and forgetful about what happened. My brother was crying too. I was glad my grandfather was there to help me.

The day of our departure, everyone was focused on making sure we had all our documents. It was difficult to say goodbye to our loved ones. We knew we might never see them again. At the airport the bag check security harassed us and tried intimidating us so we would give them bribes. They scared me the way they looked and talked to my parents. They mocked us for being refugees and leaving to America, making a mess of our packed bags in order to make us miss our flight.

My Mama took me into the bathroom and hid her cross necklace and ring in my pantyhose. The bags were thrown around, breaking the only heirloom we had of my father's mother. The airport security tried to provoke and insult my parents. They took my father into a room to strip search him. They humiliated him and threatened us in order for us to give them our jewelry and money. They thought we were taking Russian treasures to America. Knowing we were Baku refugees still they harassed us. Finally, we were let through and boarded the airplane.

The whole flight I asked my parents questions. How big is America? Will our relatives visit us? What is this food they serve to us? Are all the people on the plane refugees too? How will we know what to say to people if we don't speak English? What if we don't like it there, will we come back to Armenia? Where will we live in America? What is

Idaho? What if someone hates us in America, where will we move then? My parents were creative and answered as much as they could. Truth was, they didn't know anything either. All they had was faith and hope for a small chance for a better life for us.

My father, always certain, was now completely uncertain about what would happen next. If something goes wrong, we had no way of going back to Armenia. We only had our one way tickets to America, no way back. We had no money, not a penny to our name. We didn't speak any English. We had four large duffle bags, packed with the few belongings we had to our name. We each had a few changes of clothes, a pair of shoes, a couple of handmade pillows, a couple of traditional llama hair adiyala одеяло (blankets) our grandmother hand made for us, some dishes, few pictures of our relatives, pots and pans and a couple of translating books to help us with English. People pack more to go camping for a weekend than we had to start our new life in America.

I remember feeling lost and sad. Even though I was a young child, I still felt empty, the feeling of separation from my relatives, motherland and a life we understood. The distance was fragmenting us more deeply. It was a strange feeling of uprooting and floating into the unknown. The same feeling of loneliness I felt when my parents put me alone on the bus to leave Baku, but deeper and longer lasting. I felt the deep loss of my extended family, my language, my land and a loss of myself. I felt the sadness of my parents and being heartbroken leaving everything they knew behind. Heartbroken that our family was thrown out of our motherland. Relieved by the long struggle to keep our family alive.

    I saw tears on my Mama's cheeks, she thought I did not notice underneath her reading glasses but I felt her deep sadness. Parting with her sister, our relatives, our grandparents, not knowing if we would ever see them again. I felt sad too, and started to think of my cousins and relatives. We didn't talk about it, we just cried saying goodbye. To me, my Mama was too beautiful to cry. It was difficult to see her cry and to not know the right words to say to make her feel better.

    As the plane landed, I felt the girl I was in Armenia start to disappear. All of a sudden we did not exist; I didn't know who we were in this new land. From the plane window I saw many lights that looked so pretty below. It was New York City, and it looked like a big cake full of colorful candy and lights. I felt anxious and scared to meet everyone, new people we never knew before. For some reason I felt that everyone down there, in the city, knew we were on our way, waiting to greet us. I became nervous. What if they do not like us? Or their children, what if they don't want to play with me, will they hurt me? Would they spit on us and tell us to go away?

    Before I knew it, we were off the plane and a refugee resettlement representative greeted my parents. As they spoke and figured out details, I stood and watched the people around me. I stood very close to my dad, scared that someone would take me away. There were people going every which way. Where were they all going I wondered?

Why were they all so happy? Everyone was smiling, showing their teeth to us.

America had many different people, Asian people, Black people, people of ethnicities I never met, and they all looked beautiful. I only saw white Americans in movies, when we watched Dynasty in Russia. I thought all Americans were white and rich, didn't know it was this diverse here. The people all looked different but they all had something about them that looked the same. A sense of happiness on their face, they were smiling all the time. I saw children with laughter and happiness, being children and playing.

Our arrival didn't feel real. Hours ago we were on the other side of the world, surrounded by chaos and struggling to eat. Now we were taking our first steps in our new country. A feeling of relief surrounded our family that evening, a feeling of safety. I kept looking around to see if any of our relatives would show up, if perhaps they were on a different flight, but soon realized that it was just the four of us here in America. This made me very sad to know that everyone else was left behind.

Our case worker met us, and explained that we still have more flying to do. We were in New York but the Refugee Program was relocating us to Idaho. In New York, my parents took an oath, filled out more paperwork for our refugee status, and we were on our way to Idaho. "Idaho? I wonder what country is Idaho? What happened to us going to America?" I thought. When I woke up we had already landed in Salt Lake City, Utah to change planes again. This airplane was so much smaller than our first airplane, like a dragonfly. I looked outside and saw nothing, absolutely nothing, just fields all around.

This place was completely different from New York, there was nothing here in Idaho. There was nobody at the airport, except two workers and the people who flew in with us. "Weird! Where was everyone? Was this still America?" I was thinking. It seemed like a whole other country from New York, scary different. I felt like we were on a different planet. I became scared, thinking they sent us to another country, where there was no one, or could it be a refugee camp?

"Children remember today, September 4th 1992, 11:28 p.m. because today is the day we arrived to our new country and our new life." As he said that I looked at the clock in the car, it was 11:28 o'clock, I did not realize that we have been flying for almost 2 days now. I could smell his cigarette and I could tell he was more at ease with the way he held and smoked it. My Papa was very consistent in his gestures; I could read his body language from a distance. How he was smoking was a sign of relief, I understood that we were safe in America.

Our apartment was on the second floor. 'E2' it was marked on the door, a real door, a real apartment! Not a utility storage in a school. Without rats! Not a hiding place, but a real home. I wasn't sure if we were guests or if this was our home. My parents and the resettlement case workers walked in front of me with our duffle bags. I took my time walking up the steps, everything smelled clean and new to me. Touching the walls, the glass and staircase I traced my fingers on every detail walking up the stairs. I worried that it would not last, that we would have to move again.

Walking into a home was an unbelievable moment for me. I forgot how it felt to live in a real home. After living homeless for years it now became normal. Suddenly part of me missed our storage home back at in Armenia. This felt too new, too nice, too large for us, I became anxious about everything new around me. I looked at the door to see how strong it was, wondering if someone could break it in. I felt a sense of distrust when the case workers asked us to walk in. I was scared that we were being tricked, and about to be robbed or hurt.

When the lights were turned on I couldn't believe the room. I looked everywhere. The room was big. It was warm. It was bright. It was clean. There was some furniture. There was a window to look outside. There was water! I checked as soon as I walked into the bathroom. This was our home? How was this our home? My mind went wild, everything felt and smelled different. There was a couch covered in a blanket, a coffee table, two mismatched chairs and a lamp. The couch smelled and was covered in a blanket with three different pillows on it. On the windows hung bright, green curtains. This made me happy because green was my favorite color.

I smelled something sweet, but looking around I did not know where it was coming from. Then my eyes froze at a large bowl of candies on the coffee table. Without asking my brother what was in the other rooms, I pulled him to the bowl of colorful candy. We both looked to see if our parents were watching. Then we each picked one candy to eat. As soon as we tasted its flavor we both made twisted faces, it wasn't sweet like we expected. Mine tasted like licorice cough medicine, and my brothers tasted sour. YUCK, we were both disappointed in America's awful candy. How can candy taste like medicine in such a praised country? I tried the other colors and soon discovered that Jelly Beans were my new favorite candy.

From the side of my eyes, I spotted a small dolly on the bed. The dolly had a broken leg, but I was excited to see it there, was my first toy in years. That night felt like a lifetime, we were all in our beds and ready to sleep our first night in this new country. For the first time in years I felt safe, warm and had a smile on my face. Holding the dolly and thinking about my relatives back in Armenia, I fell asleep. That night was the first safe and warm night that I experienced since before we became refugees. Sleeping without the noise of the rats scratching our walls, without the fear of being bitten by them. I wondered, what did I dream about that night? What was my first dream in America about? I know for sure it was not a nightmare.

This is the first photo we took as a family in Twin Falls, Idaho. Pictured here are our first friends, U.S. Army Veteran John Smith and Pastor Roger Davis with The Salvation Army (United States, December 1992)

10

Culture Shock

"Something different happened to my family after we arrived to America. I thought our life would be better and it is, still there is sadness in our home."

(journal entry - age 13)

Waking up that first morning in America was surreal. Waking up in Twin Falls, Idaho - America? What kind of America is this? Where is everyone? It was a cold September morning. My Papa and Mama got us dressed and took us outside for a walk. We walked up the block to a grocery store. The doors opened on their own! With music and warmth, the store welcomed us in. There was food EVERYWHERE! Everywhere my eyes looked there was fruit, bread, vegetables, juice, meat, boxes of cookies, candy. I had never seen this much food in my life in one place. I thought to myself, this store must feed all of America. It was overwhelming to touch and smell all the food, I felt guilty because I knew how people were starving back home. It was unbelievable to me the amount of food in abundance there was in one store.

I felt guilty having all this food to choose from and eat. Everything was so perfect, every shelf full, not a single empty spot. All the fruit was so clean, so shiny, that my mouth watered at the thought of how delicious it all must taste. I looked at the people. They all looked happy. Everyone smiled at us. Why did they smile at us?

I made up my young mind and determined that Americans must just like to show their teeth to each other. I was shocked they showed their teeth to us like that. I thought it might be rude to show my teeth back. It felt awkward to me to show my teeth, something so primitive in nature, that I felt like I was growling. Why would they smile at us if they didn't know us? I stared at everyone because they were interesting to me. There was a calm on their faces, not like the worried faces I was used to seeing on the adults

I knew growing up. My parents bought a few groceries and we walked back to our apartment.

The street was quiet; we were the only ones walking. The homes were short and small, not like the tall buildings that we lived in back home. Everyone had perfect grass around their house; it was the first time I had seen grass this perfect. "Why do they have so much grass?" I thought to myself. Everything about our new home was intriguing to me. The nice doors, windows, bathroom, locks - the doorbell.

I developed a habit of flicking the lights on and off to see if they would run out of electricity. I wondered when the government would turn the power or water off. Turning the water on and watching it go, become warm, then cold, then warm again. Everything seemed so perfect in America, I was not used to this feeling. I felt anxious thinking about the possibility of us losing everything and moving again.

The people outside our apartment were friendly and happy. Nature was happy, even the animals outside seemed happy and fed. The sidewalks were happy. The buildings were happy. The cars were happy. The children were happy. The old people were happy. The air was happy. How can air feel happy? It felt happy to me! It felt safe to me. I started singing songs in Armenian again. Remembering my life in Armenia, I missed my cousins and was sad that we had to live so far away. I wished my family could all be together, and often dreamt about them at night.

Those first days we were busy with administrators, translators and lots of paperwork. My parents constantly had papers in their hands, and a translator book in their grip to attempt to communicate. We had a physical checkup at the Refugee Center and then were taken back home. The case worker gave my parents a booklet of food stamps to buy food with. Some refugees might arrive to America with a little money. However, we were not that lucky. My parents didn't have any cash on them, not even foreign currency to exchange. They sold what they could to buy our train tickets from Armenia to Moscow. Right away they had to take the first jobs offered to them. We had Medicaid, since they made very little income combined and food assistance. We were poor, for years we struggled, but my parents were determined to provide for us.

     The Refugee Center registered my brother and I to attend school at Lincoln Elementary, two blocks away from our apartment. I was scared to leave my parents, afraid I wouldn't see them again. I remember my brother and I were scared to go, thinking the kids would call us names or hurt us.

     We stood at the office as they assigned us teachers. I didn't want to let my brother go! He was in a higher grade and so we were separated, I was placed in a different classroom. I was so sad to be separated by my brother I cried. I remember walking into my classroom and all the children looking back at me. I didn't have a backpack, or a pencil or anything they had. I didn't understand the teacher or any of the children, just was sitting on a chair and trying not to cry.

Some refugees, upon relocating to America, change or adopt new names and surnames to avoid discrimination. We didn't change our names. It was embarrassing every time the teachers called my name wrong. I couldn't hide from how foreign I was. Over the years, I slowly adjusted to the new life here. I don't think we ever felt a sense of belonging as refugees in our new community. My parents experienced discrimination at their jobs and they made us feel like we didn't belong here.

I looked around and everyone looked so different than me. Different faces, different clothes, they smelled different, moved differently and they all stared at me. At lunch, I couldn't recognize the food; it smelled funny to me. I just wanted to go home, to be with my parents and brother. I hated going to school. That was, until other Refugee children moved to the same town. We would meet in our English learning class.

As I made a few new refugee friends, school life began to improve. English as a Second Language (ESL) courses were a step-by-step introduction of the American English to foreign speakers. English is a very difficult language to learn. My father was very clear in letting my brother and I know that school was our job. Education was stressed and valued in our family, and I knew that my family's life depended on how well I did in school.

Very few have the privilege of extended family support, childcare or time to attend English learning classes. When refugees arrive to America, they are expected to get to work right away. At best, refugees get a below minimum wage paying job where very little or no communication was necessary. Working 8-12 hours a day, cooking and caring for children, it was difficult to learn English.

My parents did their best to learn English. With our help and from what we learned at school, we could help get them around. For years, my parents walked around with translation books and papers with written English phrases to point to in order to communicate. Rebuilding our life was their priority, they had no other option but to work. Working two full time jobs each took our parent out of the home majority of the day. They wanted to save for a car, to save for a house, to provide us with a stable life.

I remember watching out of our apartment window my Mama walking to work every day, in the cold, in the rain, in the heat, in the snow blizzard, back and forth. We didn't have a car and the refugee center did not provide transportation to work, to doctor appointments or to shop for food. I was not happy to see my beautiful mother work like a slave. She would work long hours and then come home to clean, cook us dinner, and help us with our homework and baths. She never complained in front of us but I could see she was exhausted and depressed. My brother and I were too small to help with cooking but we helped with what we could and took turns doing chores to help our parents out. Our father too would work two full time jobs, one graveyard shift. I don't remember seeing him some weeks. We would be at school and, by the time we came home, he was away at work. No time for family time, it was America time - work, work, work.

Those first months after our arrival were very lonely for our family. We spent time sitting in our home, without transportation or, for fear of getting lost, we stayed home. After the first few weeks the refugee resettlement staff didn't check on us. Calling to speak to our family was extremely expensive and we could speak for only 5 or 10 minutes a month. We were extremely homesick. Not speaking the language made it difficult to make friends. We also didn't know who we could trust.

My parent's social life was with other refugees who just arrived. Mostly the conversations were about the violence we all survived and how each of us escaped. They assisted each other in adjusting to new jobs, homes and life in America. It felt good to be around people who understood what we lived through first hand. Overhearing their conversations over dinner or tea made me realize how important it was for all of them to share what they had survived. I realized early on that my Armenian people suffered from generational genocide, and that this was our common story.

Learning about our new country on our own was difficult for my Papa and Mama. They did not have anyone to help them with the basics of how to pay bills, fill out applications or open a bank account. They did not know what a credit score was or interest, finance and fee charges. It was easy for us to be taken advantage of because we did not know our rights or the laws here.

My parents navigated the system on their own using a translation book to communicate as best as they could. This was a very stressful time for our family, emotionally, mentally and financially. At times, my parents would become so overwhelmed with stress that they would argue and fight in front of us. There was more to worry about every day and less help from the resettlement program. The community we lived in didn't have many refugees and, without social or emotional support, we felt completely alone.

Something different happened to our family after we arrived to America. I thought our life would get better, and it did in many ways, but there was still a deep depression and sadness in our home. Our home had an emptiness, a silence that felt like a long grieving of loss. We avoided talking about our past, our sadness, like it never happened. It was too painful to relive. Our homesickness grew into depression. I thought we would forget everything that happened and we would start a new life. Our trauma and sadness followed us to our new life in America, it stayed with us, moved with us and was still inside us.

The yelling in our home was something new, we didn't have this yelling before, and now it was frequent. I could tell my parents worried, their personalities changed, they became exhausted and stressed. I feel like this country stole my parents from me. My parents became extremely overwhelmed, I stayed out of their way because I knew how stressed out they were. I didn't see my Mama smile much anymore, she kept to herself, in her deep depression.

I think back, to what we lost as a family during this fast resettlement process. My parents were happy to finally be in America, at the same time they felt desperate to rebuild our lives. I didn't want to burden my family with the confusing thoughts and feelings I was experiencing. Everything happened fast, there was no time to cope, heal or manage our trauma as a family. The resettlement program after a few weeks stopped checking in with us. We were dropped from the sky and left on our own to survive again.

We came to America as one family, but we faced individual assimilation challenges that each of us experienced alone. We were living in dual cultures, the culture at home and the American culture outside of our home. I experienced a constant tug and pull between the two. The burden of proving your Americanism while labeled as an "Other". I was either too American for my Armenian community or not American enough for my American community and it was very exhausting to try to balance.

The integration experience that my brother and I had was completely separate and different from what my parents experienced. Language was our advantage. Language was our key to exploring the culture. We became more exposed to American culture through school than our parents were in their isolated jobs and closed-off social circle. They felt they could lose us to this country. My parents worried we would lose our language, our identity, our culture in this country. We lived on two different levels of America, the one of total exploitation of the arriving refugee adults and the one of cultural separation and assimilation of their children.

11

Post-Traumatic Stress Disorder

As a child, I felt safe by ignoring what I could around me. Unsure of what was happening, or what would happen next, I learned to feel nothing. No matter how hard I try, these moments, smells, sounds, feelings and visuals that replay in my mind:

complete silence
strangers in our home
can't go to preschool
tanks in the street
crowds chanting
terror
don't sing
don't play
uncle stabbed in the head
strange child on my blanket
not sleeping in my bed
not allowed to sing
not allowed to go outside
noises outside our house
homes broken into
stabbing
dismembered people
grandfather beaten up
leaving my parents
fear
confusion
tanks running over people
where are my parents
where are we going
are we going home
adult talk

red carnations
thrown from the 8th floor
screaming in her sleep
smell of bread
cold
yelling
knives
breasts cut off
burnt alive
heads split open
rats scratching the walls
burnt human bones
be quiet
scared eyes
alone on the bus
where is my toy
where is my brother
mother busy hands
whispers at night
homelessness
freezing
rats
hunger
lice itching
waiting in the car
smell of kerosene
human feces
smell of dead rats
dark public baths
drowning
grandmother crying
my cousin yelling for her Mama

nervous
strangers
plane crash
making candles

*My Mama & my brother become United States citizens
(Boise, Idaho, 2000)*

12

I am Other

"They have boxes for people in America. White, African American, Hispanic, Island People... for us, they have the 'Other' box. I am 'Other' here. They make me 'Other' in America. 'Other' is like chair, cactus, rock... 'Other.' How can I be human as 'Other'? I don't want to live as 'Other'"

(journal entry - 14 years old)

When you are a displaced person, you do not belong anywhere, are unwanted everywhere. Unlike refugees who are protected under international law, there is no law to protect displaced people or one that defended their right to life. Both displaced people and refugees' right to life is at the mercy of someone else. Displaced, dehumanized and destabilized from the moment people are uprooted and forced out of their homes, they are in a constant, pending uncertainty. A displaced person has no face, has no land, has no name - only identified as a "conflict," or "humanitarian crisis". Displaced people are the largest invisible population on Earth. Most people do not know the difference in numbers of internationally displaced persons and the few who are lucky to be granted a refugee status. Millions never do.

When a person is a refugee, they are identified by a case, a file, a status. Their life, their future is in the hands of case workers, administrators, organizations and foreign policy. Their identity is molded by systems and institutions designed to rescue, relocate and resettle them. Truly, there is no personal identity in moments of despair, there is only the instinct to survive. The dehumanizing reality refugees endure can erode the human spirit, dissolve one's humanity and contribute to feeling of worthlessness. Leaving behind everything you identify with as "you", your family, your heritage, your home, your country, your language is extremely traumatic.

It feels like the earth beneath you falls away. I hated the feeling of constantly falling into unfamiliar and frightening places as a child. Lost in loss. The adults in my life were lost, the looks on their faces, scared, hopeless, helpless stuck in their chronic insecurity about life. Refugees are the burden population no one wants in their country. We know this feeling, it is a feeling we inherit along with our survivor's guilt. Pushed out of our home and our country we have no piece of land to call "home." My family was lucky to survive the killings and escape to a neighboring country. Arriving desperate for safety in Armenia, we were received as strangers by our own people. I felt like the planet was too crowded for us.

Armenian refugees from Baku were unwelcome, unwanted in Armenia. "Why are we so hated?" I asked my Mama and father. "We are not wanted there, we are not wanted here, what is wrong with us?" This was the first time I experienced discrimination and hostility within my own Armenian community. The only difference between us and the Armenians in Armenia, was that we were born in Baku and spoke Russian. I never understood why this rich diversity of our people was used to divide us instead of unite us. Feeling the hate of the world as a child forced me to withdraw and become invisible. At that time, I could not understand the economic, material, political and psychological factors of our situation. Still, I knew this strong hate between adults was wrong. I understood hate before I understood love.

To exist without shelter and safety is to feel like an animal, not even human. Homelessness is a most degrading and primitive state of existence. We experienced homelessness for almost four years while waiting to be granted refugee status. Living in a school storage closet was the closest I experienced to a third world prison. This place was disgusting, with rats as plump as mid-size dogs, open sewage and trash everywhere. Worse than prison. At least in prison there is guaranteed water, food, heat and plumbing.

We survived, waiting day after day, as our money ran out, kerosene ran out, food ran out and hope diminished. Waited to be vetted, at the mercy of a signature on our paperwork to be granted refugee status. The difference between staying alive and dying - a signature. At the mercy of the good hearted people of the world, we waited and prayed.

Displaced people are seen as subhuman. Our lives, our fate, our human rights negotiated as if we are disposable objects. We are seen as the problem, the burden and cause of instability. Our humanity is overshadowed by political noise and conflict debates, our human worth diminished. Instead of hating the politicians, conflicts and wars they make to create us, people hate the refugees. We are referred to as numbers, not individual human lives, but population numbers without an identity. Refugees are "Other-ed" we are the "Others" of this world.

I felt like I was not human when we lived homeless. I felt like a burden for surviving the killings in Baku, a burden for staying alive, that my family's survival was a burden on the rest of the world. I felt worthless, like an object, worthless and disposable as a child and adolescent. I felt unworthy of life, worthy only of the suffering and abuse from other people. The proof was in how we lived. It's normal to feel this despair when everything around us no longer reflects our human dignity and who we are.

I soon developed confusion and fear of identifying myself. I felt like I lost "me". I felt safer hiding my identity, hiding my past, hiding my faith, hiding my language accents. If I expressed my Christian faith as a child, I could be killed. If I expressed my Russian fluency, I could be beaten. It was never safe to be who I really was, I learned that at a very young age. I let other people tell me who I was, at school, in Armenia, in America. Surrendering to someone else telling me who I am, or giving me my new name, my life story and my new identity.

In America, there are set structures for identity, for race, color and heritage - White, African American, Hispanic, Native American, Pacific Islander. There are no identity boxes to check for people like me on application forms here. I can only mark "other" in America. Really all my life I have been an "Other" in one way or another. In my own birth country, I did not belong, persecuted because of my identity. As a displaced person, I did not belong, humiliated and dehumanized because of my identity. As a refugee, I did not belong, discriminated and persecuted because of my identity. When you do not belong, you are "other." That's how I knew, because that is what they called me.

My whole life I've been defined by someone or something other than myself. Soviet, Russian, Armenian, Bakinka, homeless, refugee, asylum seeker, resident alien - somewhere in between all these definitions I exist. My documents, status, citizenship, race, nationality and even history has been decided by something outside of me. I feel these changes happening around me, happening to me but not with my participation. I have no control over who I am in this life. They decide for me, with their papers, category boxes and signatures, they tell me who I am in this country. I feel overwhelmed by these changes, I feel hurt by these changes, I learn to detach from reality. Refugees are invisible, I am invisible. Invisible, placeless, voiceless - how can someone invisible have an identity?

My personality became unfamiliar to me, my identity felt split between traumas and cultures. Something was happening to me, inside of me, I did not recognize this person. I knew who I was in my culture, but not now. I felt as an observer, distant, out of body and detached from the changes happening to our family. Part of me was numb to thoughts or feelings I experienced. Another part of me was intensely feeling emotions of loss, fear and anxiety. Some of it was culture shock, most of it was culture clash of fitting in with who we were in this new place.

I searched for the right words to express what I was experiencing and feeling while adjusting to my new identity and life in America. Life as an "Other", not an American citizen, not a refugee - a pending other, living in the margins of this society. I understand my identity is changing. I don't have control over the changes in my life happening to me. I am in a space of no identity. The word I find accurate to give name to this space of transition, is Liminal. Liminal space is the crossing over I experienced - of leaving something behind that is true but have not yet able to replace it with anything else. When I read about this word, I knew this was me. This one word changed my life, it helped me define a space I could find myself in and experience the world from.

I am not the girl in Armenia. I can never know her again. Even my name sounds strange to me. I feel I am constantly changing into a girl I don't know. The changes to my life sculpt me without my permission. Pending documents, pending status, pending trauma and pending identity is a personal threshold refugees experience. I think people experience this liminal space in major life changes, post trauma, recovering addiction or post-divorce, when they experience the fragmentation of their identity, personality and inner self. I recognized this inner space before I knew what to call it exactly.

Liminal for me is found in that space between two uncertainties. Liminal is in the present-time stillness, far from the traumatic past and uncertain future. I have nothing else than this liminal space. I am Liminal. When my childhood memories become too intense, I close my eyes and come back to this liminal space. From this liminal space I connect to myself, to my family, the violence we survived and the trauma we continue live with. Something I was made to feel ashamed of, and humiliated for, I now feel some control and power over my life. Being stripped of all the acceptable labels that form traditional identity gives me the feeling of liberty. I do not want to live my life only as a genocide victim, or only as a genocide survivor, I want to live my life as a human.

I refused to be limited by my past or present. Forced to have an identify as an "Other", I rebelled on application forms that required me to pick a box to identify with. At school, at hospitals, even common surveys required me to choose from 5-6 box categories of identity, that would leave people like me with the "Other" box. I was told to mark "Other" in school by teachers confused about my background. I watched people mark "Other" for me when they filling out information about me. Every time I saw that box it made me feel like I didn't exist, that my Armenian ethnicity was nonexistent on this continent. If a box for me did not exist, I did not exist.

How could a country of immigrants from all over the world have only 5 "race" boxes to fit everyone in? I was jealous of my White American, Latino American and African American friends because they had a box they could mark, they belonged, and I didn't. I was introduced to Hip Hop and realized how both Latinos and Black Americans experienced similar struggles that refugees face in modern America. I learned the most about this culture's history by listening to artists like Dr. Dre, Ice Cube, Snoop Dogg, MC Lyte, Mobb Deep, Tupac, Wu-Tang Clan, Nas, Lauryn Hill, Jay-Z, Queen Latifah, KRS-One, the part of culture left out of the textbooks. Hip-Hop is America's most honest ambassador, representing the truth of its peoples' history and struggles to the world.

Hip-Hop music opened my eyes to the history of oppression, the violence, the genocide and something I didn't know anything about - racism. It takes a long time to get to know America, even longer to become aware of America's constructed racism. It's impossible to understand America without first understanding systemic racism, not everyone is prepared for that. I gained a new perspective about the suffering my family endured and it gave me new strength. I found meaning in the suffering my family endured. I am Armenian, I am proud of my Armenian ethnicity. I am a refugee, that means I am a survivor. In my suffering is my victory, my strength and my courage. That is who I am. That is my identity, not "Other."

One day, I was filling out an application form and instead of marking the "Other" box, I drew a small box underneath it and wrote in "Armenian" - then, I proudly marked my own box. It felt good not to compromise who I was or to "Other" myself. From that moment on I chose to be in control of my identity. I chose to be brave and correct people when they mispronounced my name. I chose to be the teller of my own story, the voice of my past and present. I chose to expand from the liminal space into my pure potential, and be in complete control of my life. Eventually I stopped drawing silly boxes, refused to participate in "othering" myself and stood proud in my rich heritage, journey and identity. I stopped feeling like I had to hide who I was, my faith or my history. I stopped apologizing for my survival. I stopped feeling ashamed of being a refugee. I stopped allowing the world to label me as subhuman, as "other," or as a terrorist.

Reflection after September 11, 2001

In America, the perception of Middle Eastern people (exactly like Indigenous American people) is summed up in negative, primitive stereotypes. It is a constructed prejudice, a historic lie. Middle Eastern people are beautiful. Lebanese, Persian, Israeli, Arab, Syrian, Armenian...all people. When I look in the mirror, I see ancient, majestic roots. The rich, complex history of Armenian, Persian, Byzantine, Assyrian and many long ruling kingdoms, tribes of Judea and royal roots of Kings and Queens. Not lifetimes ago, just generations ago. The pulsing birthplace of Jesus of Nazareth, also Middle Eastern, on the soil my ancestors and I called home.

My facial structure and the features I see in my reflection are reminders of Noah's Ark, reminders of the Fertile Crescent. They are reminders of the birthplace of all the world's religions, the silk trade route, where Asia, Africa and Europe meet. When I look in the mirror, I never see the ugliness of fear or terror. Rather, I see the proud birth of languages, geometry, astrology, medicine, chemistry, paper making, textiles, woven cloths, currency, music, wine, gems, spices, architecture, poetry, art, algebra, trigonometry, physics, democracy, philosophy and the first of multi-ethnic, multi-religious complex metropolitan areas. The Middle East contributed all of this, and more, to humanity. Most of these contributions were falsely attributed to Europe centuries later by those who rewrote history.

Armenians are indigenous peoples and, although our borders have been bullied around us and our ancestral territory stolen from us, our culture and pride lives on in our hearts. My great grandparents were priests, merchants and intellectuals during the 1915 Armenian Genocide, after which they were forced into exile in the Syrian desert.

Strangers in new countries, we held on to what we cherished most - our faith, our family and our Armenian identity. We know who we are regardless of whether they sent us to Argentina, Idaho or Mars. We are not terrorists. Who is exporting the wars? We are not the terrorists. Middle Eastern people are some of the most hospitable and caring people and this behavior can be seen when we express kindness towards strangers. Hosting a guest is the highest honor for a family, rich or poor. Intellectuals, teachers and spiritual leaders are highly regarded in most Middle Eastern societies as they provide wisdom to the generations who come and go. Middle Eastern culture is about honor, dignity and family, not having these three is what I believe constitutes true poverty.

In Middle Eastern culture, the best things you can wish a person is Health, Happiness and Long Life. Material wealth does not take priority over what is truly important. We are taught from childhood that all life is equal, and Mother Nature is above all, sacred. This is what belongs to God, and is to be left with as little human damage as possible. Our fathers are warriors, our mothers are generals, and our elders are our anchors in changing times. In Armenian culture, women, mothers and grandmothers are sacred at the very least. A person's solid integrity and character is worth more than gold. God is the only judge and to be flawed is to be human.

Our pride comes from our integrity and gratitude. Our honor comes from our respect for our elders and that which is sacred in this life unto the next. With or without makeup, I love my Armenian features. They remind me of who I am. My ancestors were killed for these features; the survival of the Armenian people is evident on my face. I love my Armenian features because they remind me of who I am, no matter where I am. I am proud of my Middle Eastern features because they represent deep roots of honor, civilization, and fundamental contribution to the whole world. I know who we are.

I know who I am. The lies, the political noise, the stereotypes, the denial of my people's history cannot touch me.

*Standing in the church at The Salvation Army in Twin Falls, Idaho
(February 1993)*

13

Integration

"My family is stuck in low paying jobs, we are rebuilding our lives with the crumbs of the American Dream."

(journal entry - age 14)

If you are coming to America, here is what to do first. It's not easy like people imagine life to be here. It is a big and beautiful country, but it can be very lonely for us refugees. My parents are working extremely hard, two jobs each to survive here. They do not have time to learn the language and cannot find better jobs. I am learning English so I can have a good job to help my parents. Some people who go to school and learn the English language find better jobs. The Refugee Center doesn't allow my parents to go to school, they said they need to go to work. My parents are happy to have jobs but they are more educated than the jobs they put them in.

Be prepared to live on your own soon after you arrive and don't expect anyone to help teach you about this Country. If you are a refugee and waiting to come to America, start learning the English language before you come here. You must learn the language. Language will open every door for you in America. American English is spoken differently than it is written, people don't speak like the grammar rules dictate. You have to learn the slang too. Refugees who know a little English get better jobs here. For adults, learning English is very difficult, but possible.

For us refugee children, learning English was easy. All our regular friends spoke English. I was learning conversational English so I would interpret for my parents everywhere. Every refugee family has an interpreter, it's the child in the family that knows English better than the rest. My writing and reading in English was weaker, as it is much more difficult to read and write the language than to speak it. Learning to speak English gave my brother and I an advantage over our parents in American society, especially because our English skills were valuable during parent teacher conferences, where we were the interpreters.

You should try to hide your accent. My parents have very bad accents. My brother has one too. I have one too but I am learning to say words better, like my American friends. I see how people look at people who speak with funny accents, they judge them. I like hearing accents, I don't notice my own, but other people do. If you have the highest education and have an accent, people still think you are uneducated. Accents are bad to your life here. Learn the language, and learn to control your accent.

Most refugees are working as janitors, dishwashers, cooks, housekeepers, factory workers or taxi drivers. This is where we all end up, even if we are doctors, teachers, engineers or nuclear physicist. We begin at the very bottom in this country. It doesn't matter who you were back home. My parents are both working lowest paying jobs, smelling chemicals and hurting their back, because they don't speak English. We do not have a chance to step ahead in America like this. Our opportunities are at the very bottom of this society, the crumbs are for us.

If you don't know English or Spanish, it's a complete communication disability. The pressure to get off of the refugee program makes it impossible to go to school to learn English. You have to work right away and pay back your airplane tickets. My parents explain to me that we (refugees) are the new slaves in America, relocated to fill lowest paying jobs no one else wants to work. It is designed for us to work these jobs and have very little chance to climb up. Why else do they hurry us so fast to employment, knowing we will forever be illiterate and stuck in factory work, unless we learn this language.

My family is stuck in low paying jobs, we are rebuilding our lives with the crumbs of the American Dream. My parents are making this sacrifice to provide a better opportunity for my brother and I. They remind me every day to study and take school serious so we can have better lives here. The burdens of a better future are on my brother and I. Refugee parents stress to their children over and again, "We came to this country for you, so that you can have a better opportunity for your life, I will clean, make beds, break my back and wash toilets so that you have a better life in this country." Our parents pay with their health and hard labor to rebuild our life in this country.

For many refugees, children and adults, memory and learning is challenging because of the trauma and their mental health. In my culture mental health is taboo, we don't talk about it. Survivors feel wrong, guilty or ashamed to talk about their experienced violence, suffering and abuse. When we say "mental health" people in my community think you are coo-coo-looney or talking about someone crazy. Mental health is a shameful and hush-hush conversation. This cultural stigma discourages family members and the people we love from connecting with professionals. When we moved to a new continent, a new country, our past mental stress and trauma followed us.

Post-Traumatic Stress Disorder is real. Maybe not for everyone, but a high number of refugees live with PTSD. PTSD is real in War Veterans, why would anyone think it was not as real in war civilians? The best decision you can make, for your quality of life and wellbeing is (when you are ready) to address your PTSD. It doesn't go away on its own, and can become worse with time. In children it can cause developmental problems, and even surface as physical illness. PTSD affects everything from ability to learn, sleep, work, live, coping with future conflict, sense of self, stress to forming lasting relationships. I suffered with Chronic PTSD all through my childhood and was not aware of what these symptoms were until my late teens. For the majority of my life, I thought the symptoms were simply part of my personality.

My entire family showed strong signs and symptoms of PTSD. Our faith was not enough to rescue us from the deep rooted mental trauma. We spend many years hurting together. I am grateful to be one of the few displaced people who attained a refugee status and was relocated to safety. I am grateful for my family and to have a second chance at life in this beautiful country. However, living with trauma as a child is not living. Reliving your trauma every day, isolated and marginalized in your adoptive community, is not living. Feeling depressed and suicidal is not living. Experiencing flashbacks, symptoms of PTSD is not living. War kills childhood, everything else can be rebuilt.

Refugee children and children of war need to be healed, re-humanized, stabilized and provided with coping techniques for their healthy emotional, mental, social and psychological development. Most of their parents are suffering from chronic PTSD as well, and cannot cope with their own trauma let alone their children's wounds. I struggled with symptoms I could not understand, I self-medicated to deal with them. It took me 18 years to identify, understand and manage my flashbacks, triggers, nightmares, eating disorders, hyper panic attacks, anxiety and survivor's guilt. I believe the last stage of healing is using what you survived to help other people. I advocate the importance of rescuing the whole human, not just the physical person. Healing refugee men, women and children emotionally, mentally and psychologically, for a whole human and healthy integration into a new society.

As part of the refugee resettlement program, arriving families should be connected with opportunities for individual or family therapy. Every family is different, every culture is different, still the opportunity for managing PTSD should be part of the resettlement program, following their arrival. For children especially, creative art, or play therapy to help cope with childhood trauma is important. Traditional counseling can be difficult due to language barriers. I discovered Eye Movement Desensitization and Reprocessing (EMDR) therapy to manage my PTSD. EMDR could be self-administered and was possible even with the challenge of language barriers. There are many different holistic pathways for addressing trauma in refugees and survivors of war. I suggest providing information in the home language of the family, to help parents identify PTSD and other behavioral, emotional, mental and physical symptoms of trauma in their children.

Assimilation can take generations, the stress of assimilating without the proper emotional support can further compound trauma. Prolonged or untreated, PTSD can contribute to major problems in life, including but not limited to: chronic depression, lifelong illness, cycles of violence, domestic violence, schizophrenia and suicide. We have to care about the mental well-being of the people we are rescuing. Organic integration is prioritizing the emotional and mental, post trauma wellbeing of the men, women and children we integrate into a new country. Compassionate response should mean following up with them over several months and years after arrival, in support of their integration to their new life in America.

Adoptive communities have a major influence in the quality of the life refugees experience during their resettlement. In most communities, refugees are the invisible people on the fringe of the community, excluded and without a voice. When my family arrived in Twin Falls, we had a very difficult time fitting in and rebuilding our life. Almost nobody in our adoptive community was aware of the refugee resettlement program hosted by the local community college. That's how irrelevant and invisible we refugees are, lowest class in a caste system. Our only value was in the labor we provided, and the sole focus of the refugee resettlement program was to quickly link refugees to a low wage job.

Isolated from the rest of the community made it difficult to learn about our new country. Most refugees stay close to their cultural and sub-cultural communities. My family was blessed to meet a woman who invited us to The

Salvation Army a few blocks from our apartment. After we started attending the local Salvation Army we started to interact with Americans and making friends with them. The local pastors saw the need to facilitate the large growing population of Russian and Armenian speaking refugees, and hosted prayer and Bible study in our native languages. This made us feel welcomed and accepted by our American friends.

Interacting with Americans is very important to refugees. It can be hard for refugees to trust or connect with people after everything they have experienced. In learning about a new country, and starting a new life here, it's important to step out of the comforts of your own community and interact with Americans. Before we made friends, we were very lonely and isolated. My family was received with great compassion by the local Salvation Army. Our first winter in America they surprised us with a Christmas tree and taught our family about the tradition of American Christmas. The American friends we made at our church helped us with filling out paperwork, and educated us about credit score and making major purchases. They explained the culture to us and strange traditions and holidays we didn't understand like Halloween and St. Patrick's Day.

The friendships we eventually formed helped us cope with the stress of adjusting to a new life and identity. Our American friends appreciated learning about our culture and shared their empathy for our trauma. Over time, we built trust and understood each other. When our parents were busy working, our American friends helped us with our homework and took us on adventures. At the community level, we still felt like outsiders but, when we were without friends, we were made to feel like we belonged. Interacting with local people can help refugees learn the language (the way Americans speak it), learn the culture, and cope with feeling depressed, homesick and culture shocked. Sharing your story (when you are ready) with people can relieve the burden of bearing your suffering alone.

I wish my family shared our survivor story more, I wish we talked about it. I wish we were connected with professionals to learn to manage our traumatic memory and symptoms. We did not have the awareness or information about resources available to address our mental wellness. My parents were too busy keeping a roof over our head and food on the table. I think about the quality of life we lost living with PTSD after arriving to America. What we experienced, forever altered our health and our family identity. What I experienced as a child forever altered me, my health and my Liminal identity.

Refugees, unlike immigrants, do not choose to leave their country for a better life, they are forced to leave everything and flee. This country saved my family's life. The day I arrived in America was my second birthday. After surviving a genocide, a natural disaster, and homelessness, I deeply feel that every moment of life after that is extra. Every day is extra. Every breath is extra. This country saved my family's life. The rest is up to us. The rest is up to me. We are victors, not victims of our past.

Me while re-visiting the school storage we lived in in Yegvard, Armenia (2005)

My brother in front of the school storage, our old place of shelter in Yegvard
(2005, Yegvard, Armenia)

Made in the USA
San Bernardino, CA
24 June 2020

74069811R00100